IN THE CHECKLIST OF LIFE

A "Working Book"
To Help You Live and Leave This Life!

SECOND EDITION

Lynn McPhelimy

In The Checklist of Life
by Lynn McPhelimy

Published by
AAIP Publishing Co. LLC
P.O. Box 102
Rockfall, CT 06481

For information and ordering, contact: AAIP Publishing Co. LLC, P.O. Box 102, Rockfall, CT 06481
Telephone: (860) 343-7231 • Toll-free: 1-888-800-6446 • Fax: (860) 346-7822 • Website: http://www.checklistoflife.com

Second Edition

ISBN 0-9657843-5-5

Printed in the United States of America.

The reader is urged to consult legal counsel regarding any legal issues or questions that topics in this book may cover.
No part of this book should serve as a legal document.

This book is dedicated to my parents,

Ellyn and Joe

What I wouldn't do to have just five more minutes with you…

ACKNOWLEDGMENTS

In My Checklist of Life

I am blessed to have

Martin, Caitlin and Colin

my family

and my friends.

Death is certain.

Life is not.

Death is not optional.
Death is natural.

So why not plan for the celebration of your life?

This "working book" will help you.

It's easy.
It's comforting.
It's a way of helping you live and leave this life.

It's good for you.
It's good for your family.
It's good for your friends.
It's even good for your pets.

TABLE OF CONTENTS

IT ALL STARTED WITH THE SEPTIC TANK…

I knew what my parents wanted.

We had some time to plan.

They both had terminal cancers – at the same time. They did everything together…even that.

I had always had hope. Perhaps, if we didn't talk about it, it wouldn't happen. After all, I needed them to be at my wedding. But, only time would tell.

In the meantime, over a cup of coffee and there were many…my mother and I would talk. More accurately, she would talk and I would listen.

> "This is what I want…" she would say, "first, no open casket."

My heart sank. Okay, whatever you say. As time went on, her list went on. And, as time went on, it got easier. She finished with "Don't cry for me. I've lived a full life. I have put myself in God's hands. If I can, I'll help you. I'll be right there beside you."

My father had things that he needed to get organized–not on the spiritual plane–but, on the practical plane. His "let's talk" chat centered around the septic tank…

> "You know when I'm gone, I don't want the yard all dug up when you're looking for the septic tank. So here is this little map."

The map was hand-drawn and the specs were exact.

With these words of parental wisdom, I have put together this "working book."

The wonderful thing about this working book is that you have the time to change and rearrange…go a step back in order to take a better step forward.

It will be okay.

JUST THE FACTS

Full Name: _____

Birthplace City: _____ State: _____ County: _____ Country: _____

Date of Birth: _____

Social Security Number: _____

Residence Established: _____

City: _____ County: _____ Country: _____

Name of Spouse or Significant Other: _____

Employer *(or retired from)*: _____

Street: _____

City: _____ State: _____ Zip: _____

County: _____ Country: _____

JUST THE FACTS

Birth Certificate is located: _____

Marriage Certificate is located: _____

Passport Number: _____ Location: _____

Religious Denomination: _____

Religious Services attended at: _____

Medicare Number: _____

Medicaid Number: _____

Name of Father: _____

His Place of Birth: _____

Name of Mother: _____

Mother's Maiden Name: _____

Her Place of Birth: _____

JUST THE FACTS

DOCTOR:

Name: _____

Street: _____

City: _____ State:_____ Zip: _____

Phone: _____

DOCTOR:

Name: _____

Street: _____

City: _____ State: _____ Zip: _____

Phone: _____

PHARMACY:

Name: _____

Street: _____

City: _____ State: _____ Zip: _____

Phone: _____

LAWYER:

Name: _____ Phone: _____

Firm: _____

Address: _____

ACCOUNTANT:

Name: _____ Phone: _____

Firm: _____

Address: _____

FINANCIAL ADVISOR:

Name: _____ Phone: _____

Firm: _____

Address: _____

IF YOU ARE A VETERAN, PLEASE COMPLETE THIS SECTION:

Name of War: _____ Serial Number: _____

Date of and Place of Induction: _____

Date and Place of Discharge: _____

Branch of Service: _____ Rank at Discharge: _____

Discharge Papers can be found: _____

NUMBERS, NUMBERS AND MORE NUMBERS

Death is only a larger kind of going abroad.

Samuel Butler (1835-1902)

IMPORTANT BANKING/CREDIT UNION INFORMATION

· The wild goose chase – where, oh where, are your accounts now?

· Don't let valuables in safe deposit boxes go unclaimed.

· Don't let the location of your savings and checking accounts be a mystery.

· It will be necessary to clean up unpaid bills and close out accounts before any distribution of funds can be made.

· Make it easy and efficient.

ACCOUNTS:

Bank/Credit Union Name:_____ Branch: _____

Address: _____

Phone Number and Contact: _____

Savings Account Number: _____ Savings Account Number:_____

Savings Account Number: _____ Savings Account Number: _____

Checking Account Number: _____ Checking Account Number: _____

Money Market Account:_____ Money Market Account: _____

Money Market Account: _____ Money Market Account: _____

Certificate of Deposit: _____ Certificate of Deposit: _____

Certificate of Deposit: _____ Certificate of Deposit: _____

Safe Deposit Box: ☐ yes   ☐ no   Key Number:_____ Location: _____

ADDITIONAL BANKING/CREDIT UNION INFORMATION

ACCOUNTS:

Bank/Credit Union Name:_____ Branch: _____

Address: _____

Phone Number and Contact: _____

Savings Account Number: _____ Savings Account Number:_____

Savings Account Number: _____ Savings Account Number: _____

Checking Account Number: _____ Checking Account Number: _____

Money Market Account:_____ Money Market Account: _____

Money Market Account: _____ Money Market Account: _____

Certificate of Deposit: _____ Certificate of Deposit: _____

Certificate of Deposit: _____ Certificate of Deposit: _____

Safe Deposit Box: ☐ yes   ☐ no   Key Number:_____ Location: _____

Other Banking Information:

IMPORTANT BANKING/CREDIT UNION INFORMATION

ACCOUNTS:

Bank/Credit Union Name:_____ Branch: _____

Address: _____

Phone Number and Contact: _____

Savings Account Number: _____ Savings Account Number:_____

Savings Account Number: _____ Savings Account Number: _____

Checking Account Number: _____ Checking Account Number: _____

Money Market Account:_____ Money Market Account: _____

Money Market Account: _____ Money Market Account: _____

Certificate of Deposit: _____ Certificate of Deposit: _____

Certificate of Deposit: _____ Certificate of Deposit: _____

Safe Deposit Box: ☐ yes   ☐ no   Key Number:_____ Location:_____

Other Banking Information:

ACCOUNTS:

Bank/Credit Union Name:_____ Branch: _____

Address: _____

Phone Number and Contact: _____

Savings Account Number: _____ Savings Account Number:_____

Savings Account Number: _____ Savings Account Number: _____

Checking Account Number: _____ Checking Account Number: _____

Money Market Account:_____ Money Market Account: _____

Money Market Account: _____ Money Market Account: _____

Certificate of Deposit: _____ Certificate of Deposit: _____

Certificate of Deposit: _____ Certificate of Deposit: _____

Safe Deposit Box: ☐ yes   ☐ no   Key Number:_____ Location: _____

Other Banking Information:

IMPORTANT INSURANCE STUFF

(Life, Health, Medical, Disability, Homeowners, Automotive...)

INSURANCE POLICIES:

Insurance Company: _____

Address: _____

Phone Number and Contact: _____

Account Type/Number: _____

Amount of Insurance: _____

Account Type/Number: _____

Amount of Insurance: _____

INSURANCE POLICIES:

Insurance Company: _____

Address: _____

Phone Number and Contact: _____

Account Type/Number: _____

Amount of Insurance: _____

Account Type/Number: _____

Amount of Insurance: _____

MORE IMPORTANT INSURANCE STUFF

(Life, Health, Medical, Disability, Homeowners, Automotive…)

INSURANCE POLICIES:

Insurance Company: _____

Address: _____

Phone Number and Contact: _____

Account Type/Number: _____

Amount of Insurance: _____

Account Type/Number: _____

Amount of Insurance: _____

INSURANCE POLICIES:

Insurance Company: _____

Address: _____

Phone Number and Contact: _____

Account Type/Number: _____

Amount of Insurance: _____

Account Type/Number: _____

Amount of Insurance: _____

MORE IMPORTANT INSURANCE STUFF

(Life, Health, Medical, Disability, Homeowners, Automotive…)

INSURANCE POLICIES:

Insurance Company: _____

Address: _____

Phone Number and Contact: _____

Account Type/Number: _____

Amount of Insurance: _____

Account Type/Number: _____

Amount of Insurance: _____

INSURANCE POLICIES:

Insurance Company: _____

Address: _____

Phone Number and Contact: _____

Account Type/Number: _____

Amount of Insurance: _____

Account Type/Number: _____

Amount of Insurance: _____

OTHER INSURANCE INFORMATION:

CHARGE CARD INFORMATION

(MasterCard, Visa, American Express, Discover, Department Stores...)

CHARGE CARD:

Company: _____

Address: _____

Phone Number: _____

Account Number: _____

CHARGE CARD:

Company: _____

Address: _____

Phone Number: _____

Account Number: _____

CHARGE CARD:

Company: _____

Address: _____

Phone Number: _____

Account Number: _____

MORE CREDIT CARD INFORMATION

CHARGE CARD:

Company: _____

Address: _____

Phone Number: _____

Account Number: _____

CHARGE CARD:

Company: _____

Address: _____

Phone Number: _____

Account Number: _____

CHARGE CARD:

Company: _____

Address: _____

Phone Number: _____

Account Number: _____

INVESTMENTS: STOCKS, BONDS AND MUTUAL FUNDS

STOCK BROKER:

Name: _____ Phone: _____

Firm: _____

Address: _____

FINANCIAL ADVISOR:

Name: _____ Phone: _____

Firm: _____

Address: _____

PORTFOLIO:

_____

_____

_____

_____

_____

_____

_____

_____

INVESTMENTS: STOCKS, BONDS AND MUTUAL FUNDS

PORTFOLIO:

_____

_____

_____

_____

_____

_____

_____

_____

_____

OTHER INFORMATION:

RETIREMENT INVESTMENTS

IRAs: (Company Name, Address, Account Number)

_____

_____

_____

_____

_____

_____

_____

ANNUITIES: (Company Name, Address, Account Number)

_____

_____

_____

_____

_____

_____

_____

RETIREMENT INVESTMENTS

KEOGHS: (Company Name, Address, Account Number)

_____

_____

_____

_____

_____

401(K) PLANS: (Company Name, Address, Account Number)

_____

_____

_____

_____

_____

EMPLOYEE STOCK OPTION PLAN (ESOP): (Company Name, Address, Account Number)

_____

_____

_____

_____

THE BENEFIT CORNER: SOCIAL SECURITY AND PENSIONS

SOCIAL SECURITY BENEFITS:

☐ Disabililty Benefits: _____

_____

☐ Dependents' Benefits: _____

_____

☐ Retirement Benefits: _____

_____

☐ Survivors' Benefits: _____

_____

Social Security Office:

Contact: _____

Street:_____ City:_____ State:_____ Zip:_____

Telephone Number:_____

PENSIONS:

☐ **Civil Service:** _____

Contact: _____

Street:_____ City:_____ State:_____ Zip:_____

Telephone Number: _____

☐ **Veterans' Administration Benefits:**

Contact: _____

Street:_____ City:_____ State: _____ Zip:_____

Telephone Number: _____

☐ **Private Employer:** _____

Contact:_____

Street: _____ City: _____ State : _____ Zip:_____

Telephone Number: _____

Other Information:

OTHER AGREEMENTS: WHAT OTHERS OWE YOU...

☐ Money:_____ ☐ Written Contract ☐ Oral Agreement

☐ Object:_____ ☐ Written Contract ☐ Oral Agreement

☐ Object:_____ ☐ Written Contract ☐ Oral Agreement

☐ Other:_____ ☐ Written Contract ☐ Oral Agreement

Who: _____

Street:_____ City:_____State:_____ Zip:_____

County: _____ Country: _____

Telephone Number: _____

Important Information:

_____

_____

_____

_____

_____

_____

_____

_____

OTHER AGREEMENTS: WHAT OTHERS OWE YOU...

☐ Money:_____ ☐ Written Contract ☐ Oral Agreement

☐ Object:_____ ☐ Written Contract ☐ Oral Agreement

☐ Object:_____ ☐ Written Contract ☐ Oral Agreement

☐ Other: _____ ☐ Written Contract ☐ Oral Agreement

Who: _____

Street:_____ City:_____ State:_____ Zip:_____

County: _____ Country: _____

Telephone Number: _____

Important Information:

_____

_____

_____

_____

_____

_____

_____

THE MATERIAL WORLD

We are but tenants, and…
shortly the great landlord will give us notice that our lease has expired.

Joseph Jefferson
(Inscription on his monument at Sandwich, Cape Cod)

REAL ESTATE: NEAR AND FAR

Over the years, you may have purchased and still own a mobile home, a condo, a vacation home, a time-share property, a co-op, a single family/multi-family residence or some commercial property or even some land not yet developed.

PRIMARY RESIDENCE:

Location: Street: _____

City: _____ State: _____ Zip: _____

County: _____ Country: _____

☐ **Own**   Deed is located: _____

☐ **Bank/Mortgage Company**

Name: _____ Branch: _____

Street: _____ City: _____ State: _____ Zip: _____

Contact: _____ Phone: _____

☐ **Rent**

Landlord Name/Property Manager: _____

Company: _____

Street: _____ City: _____ State: _____ Zip: _____

Phone: _____

Other Information:

REAL ESTATE: NEAR AND FAR

☐ **Time-Share**   ☐ **Vacation Home**   ☐ **Mobile Home**   ☐ **Condo**   ☐ **Co-op**   ☐ **Multi-Family**

☐ **Commercial**   ☐ **Land**   ☐ **Other** _____

Location: Street: _____

City: _____ State: _____ Zip: _____

County: _____ Country: _____

☐ **Own**   Deed is located: _____

☐ **Bank/Mortgage Company**

Name: _____ Branch: _____

Street: _____ City: _____ State: _____ Zip: _____

Contact: _____ Phone: _____

☐ **Rent** as source of income

Property Manager: _____

Company: _____

Street: _____ City: _____ State: _____ Zip: _____

Phone: _____

Other Information:

REAL ESTATE: NEAR AND FAR

☐ **Time-Share**   ☐ **Vacation Home**   ☐ **Mobile Home**   ☐ **Condo**   ☐ **Co-op**   ☐ **Multi-Family**

☐ **Commercial**   ☐ **Land**   ☐ **Other** _____

Location: Street: _____

City: _____ State: _____ Zip: _____

County: _____ Country: _____

☐ **Own**   Deed is located: _____

☐ **Bank/Mortgage Company**

Name: _____ Branch: _____

Street: _____ City: _____ State: _____ Zip: _____

Contact: _____ Phone: _____

☐ **Rent** as source of income

Property Manager: _____

Company: _____

Street: _____ City: _____ State: _____ Zip: _____

Phone: _____

Other Information:

REAL ESTATE: NEAR AND FAR

☐ **Time-Share**   ☐ **Vacation Home**   ☐ **Mobile Home**   ☐ **Condo**   ☐ **Co-op**   ☐ **Multi-Family**

☐ **Commercial**   ☐ **Land**   ☐ **Other** _____

Location: Street: _____

City: _____ State: _____ Zip: _____

County: _____ Country: _____

☐ **Own**   Deed is located: _____

☐ **Bank/Mortgage Company**

Name: _____ Branch: _____

Street: _____ City: _____ State: _____ Zip: _____

Contact: _____ Phone: _____

☐ **Rent** as source of income

Property Manager: _____

Company: _____

Street: _____ City: _____ State: _____ Zip: _____

Phone: _____

Other Information:

REAL ESTATE: NEAR AND FAR

☐ **Time-Share**   ☐ **Vacation Home**   ☐ **Mobile Home**   ☐ **Condo**   ☐ **Co-op**   ☐ **Multi-Family**

☐ **Commercial**   ☐ **Land**   ☐ **Other** _____

Location: Street: _____

City: _____ State: _____ Zip: _____

County: _____ Country: _____

☐ **Own**   Deed is located: _____

☐ **Bank/Mortgage Company**

Name: _____ Branch: _____

Street: _____ City: _____ State: ____ Zip: ____

Contact: _____ Phone: _____

☐ **Rent** as source of income

Property Manager: _____

Company: _____

Street: _____ City: _____ State: ____ Zip: ____

Phone: _____

Other Information:

REAL ESTATE: NEAR AND FAR

☐ **Time-Share** ☐ **Vacation Home** ☐ **Mobile Home** ☐ **Condo** ☐ **Co-op** ☐ **Multi-Family**

☐ **Commercial** ☐ **Land** ☐ **Other** _____

Location: Street: _____

City: _____ State: _____ Zip: _____

County: _____ Country: _____

☐ **Own** Deed is located: _____

☐ **Bank/Mortgage Company**

Name: _____ Branch: _____

Street: _____ City: _____ State: _____ Zip: _____

Contact: _____ Phone: _____

☐ **Rent** as source of income

Property Manager: _____

Company: _____

Street: _____ City: _____ State: _____ Zip: _____

Phone: _____

Other Information:

IMPORTANT TO THE WELL-BEING OF THE HOME

Very often, one person in the house handles the technical difficulties that may arise.

Do you know the intimate details of the furnace, the toilet, the dishwasher?

Share the knowledge.

IMPORTANT NAMES AND NUMBERS:

Plumber: _____ Phone: _____

Electrician: _____ Phone: _____

Well/Septic Experts: _____ Phone: _____

Handyman: _____ Phone: _____

☐ **Oil:**   ☐ **Gas Delivery:**

Company: _____

Street: _____ City: _____ State: _____ Zip: _____

Contact: _____ Phone: _____

Rubbish Removal: _____ Phone: _____

Others: _____ Phone: _____

_____ Phone: _____

_____ Phone: _____

...THE WELL-BEING OF THE HOME

HELPFUL HINTS WHEN DEALING WITH:

Fuses/Circuit Breakers: _____

_____

Where to turn water off: _____

_____

Furnace/Hot Water Heater:_____

_____

Other things about the home that only you would know...and others really need to know:

_____

_____

_____

_____

It wouldn't hurt to take a tour of your house to see what's what and where it is and what in heaven's name does it do?

THINGS TO KEEP THE YARD SEASONALLY HAPPY

SPRING CHORES regarding the lawn, trees, shrubs and flowers and vegetable garden:

_____

_____

_____

_____

SUMMER CHORES regarding the lawn, trees, shrubs and flowers and vegetable garden:

_____

_____

_____

_____

AUTUMNAL CHORES regarding the lawn, trees, shrubs and flowers and vegetable garden:

_____

_____

_____

_____

WINTER CHORES regarding the lawn, trees, shrubs and flowers and vegetable garden:

_____

_____

_____

_____

OTHER THINGS TO KEEP THE YARD SEASONALLY HAPPY:

LAWN CARE/LANDSCAPER:

Name: _____

Address: _____ Phone: _____

SNOW CARE:

Name: _____

Address:_____ Phone:_____

TOOLS/EQUIPMENT:

Can be found:

Who has borrowed what:

VEHICLES: LAND, SEA AND AIR

☐ **Car/Truck**   ☐ **Recreational Vehicle**   ☐ **Boat**   ☐ **Plane**   ☐ **Other** _____

Year: _____ Make: _____ Model: _____

    Description: _____

    Located: _____

☐ **Own**   Title: _____

☐ **Leasing Company**

Name: _____ Branch: _____

Street: _____City:_____ State: _____ Zip: _____

Contact: _____ Phone: _____

To whom shall it go:

Name:_____

Street:_____City:_____State: _____ Zip:_____

Phone:_____

Other Information:

VEHICLES: LAND, SEA AND AIR

☐ **Car/Truck**　　☐ **Recreational Vehicle**　　☐ **Boat**　　☐ **Plane**　　☐ **Other** _____

Year: _____ Make: _____ Model: _____

　　　Description: _____

　　　Located: _____

☐ **Own**　　　　　Title: _____

☐ **Leasing Company**

Name: _____ Branch: _____

Street: _____ City: _____ State: _____ Zip: _____

Contact: _____ Phone: _____

To whom shall it go:

Name: _____

Street: _____ City: _____ State: _____ Zip: _____

Phone: _____

Other Information:

VEHICLES: LAND, SEA AND AIR

☐ **Car/Truck**   ☐ **Recreational Vehicle**   ☐ **Boat**   ☐ **Plane**   ☐ **Other** _____

Year: _____ Make: _____ Model: _____

Description: _____

Located: _____

☐ **Own**   Title: _____

☐ **Leasing Company**

Name: _____ Branch: _____

Street: _____ City: _____ State: _____ Zip: _____

Contact: _____ Phone: _____

To whom shall it go:

Name: _____

Street: _____ City: _____ State: _____ Zip: _____

Phone: _____

Other Information:

VEHICLES: LAND, SEA AND AIR

☐ **Car/Truck**   ☐ **Recreational Vehicle**   ☐ **Boat**   ☐ **Plane**   ☐ **Other** _____

Year: _____ Make: _____ Model: _____

Description: _____

Located: _____

☐ **Own**   Title: _____

☐ **Leasing Company**

Name: _____ Branch: _____

Street: _____ City: _____ State: _____ Zip: _____

Contact: _____ Phone: _____

To whom shall it go:

Name: _____

Street: _____ City: _____ State: _____ Zip: _____

Phone: _____

Other Information:

THINGS TO KEEP THE VEHICLES SEASONALLY HAPPY

SPRING DUTIES regarding the well-being of the vehicles:

_____

_____

_____

_____

SUMMER DUTIES regarding the well-being of the vehicles:

_____

_____

_____

_____

AUTUMNAL DUTIES regarding the well-being of the vehicles:

_____

_____

_____

_____

WINTER DUTIES regarding the well-being of the vehicles:

_____

_____

_____

_____

OTHER THINGS TO KEEP THE VEHICLES SEASONALLY HAPPY:

Favorite Mechanic:

Name:_____

Address:_____

Phone:_____

Favorite Garage:

Name:_____

Address: _____

Phone:_____

The titles to the vehicles can be found:

_____

Other important papers can be found:

_____

_____

_____

Other information:

STUFF AND THE STORY BEHIND IT

When taking a look around yourself, you undoubtedly are surrounded by stuff.

You've collected it over the years or more accurately…it has collected you.

Some stuff has great meaning.
Some has little meaning.
And some has no meaning but a lot of dust.

Nobody knows but you. But now here's your chance to share.

ITEM	DESCRIPTION/LOCATION	SPECIAL MEANING	TO WHOM SHALL IT GO

MORE STUFF AND THE STORY BEHIND IT

ITEM	DESCRIPTION/LOCATION	SPECIAL MEANING	TO WHOM SHALL IT GO

MORE STUFF AND THE STORY BEHIND IT

ITEM	DESCRIPTION/LOCATION	SPECIAL MEANING	TO WHOM SHALL IT GO

MORE STUFF AND THE STORY BEHIND IT

ITEM	DESCRIPTION/LOCATION	SPECIAL MEANING	TO WHOM SHALL IT GO

So, when the time comes, it will be okay for the big tag sale sign to go up and have a hoard of strangers come pawing through your stuff because…anything you valued and loved will already be in its new home with its rightful new owner.

HIDING PLACES: WE ALL HAVE THEM…BUT WHERE ARE THEY?

This is to let someone know that hidden away in that drawer…or on that top shelf is…

Let someone know where to find those things that were squirreled away and might be forgotten.

The keys to the safe deposit box(es) are:

The combinations to the locks are:

OR – Person who knows where you may have put keys and/or combination information:

Name: _____

Address: _____

City: _____ State: _____ Country: _____

Phone: _____

MORE ON THOSE HIDING PLACES:

REMEMBER WHEN...?

To live in the hearts we leave behind is not to die.

Thomas Campbell (Hallowed Ground)

THE MEMORY BANK

When a friend of ours died suddenly, leaving three small children, my eight-year-old son worried about the children forgetting their mom. "All they have left of her are memories," he said.

As time moves on, it is too easy to forget those little things.

Memories are irreplaceable.

Make your deposits regularly.

YOUR MOTHER AND FATHER:

What are some of the memories that you have when your mind wanders back to holidays, vacations, times together, times apart, family rituals, family traditions…

THE MEMORY BANK

YOUR MOTHER AND FATHER:

THE MEMORY BANK

YOUR CHILDREN:

What are the special times that come to mind when you think about your children?

What are some of the memories that you have when your mind wanders back to holidays, vacations, times together, times apart, family rituals, family traditions…

_____

_____

_____

_____

_____

_____

_____

_____

_____

_____

_____

YOUR CHILDREN:

_____

_____

_____

_____

_____

_____

_____

_____

_____

_____

_____

_____

_____

THE MEMORY BANK

SIGNIFICANT OTHER (Husband, wife, lover, partner-for-life):

Ships passing in the night – running to work, running to meetings.
We all do it…whatever it takes to get to the next day.

So what would your significant other remember?
      You paid the bills on time?
      You belonged to a number of organizations?
      Supper was or was not on the table every night?

Or will he or she remember the times you broke into spontaneous…laughing in the kitchen?

What are some of the memories you have when your mind wanders back to holidays, vacations, times together, times apart, times that made the two of you stronger…?

_____

_____

_____

_____

_____

_____

_____

_____

YOUR SIGNIFICANT OTHER:

THE MEMORY BANK

FAMILY:

SIBLINGS–BROTHERS AND SISTERS

Forget the rivalry. What are some of the memories that you have when your mind wanders back to holidays, vacations, times together, times apart, family rituals, family traditions…

_____

_____

_____

_____

_____

_____

_____

_____

_____

_____

_____

FAMILY:
SIBLINGS – BROTHERS AND SISTERS

THE MEMORY BANK

THE GRAND FAMILY:

THE GRANDPARENTS

This is your history. Recall their stories. Recall your times with them.

_____

_____

_____

_____

_____

_____

_____

_____

_____

_____

_____

_____

THE GRAND FAMILY:

THE GRANDPARENTS

THE MEMORY BANK

THE GRAND FAMILY:

THE GRANDPARENTS

This is your history. Recall their stories. Recall your times with them.

THE GRAND FAMILY:

THE GRANDPARENTS

THE MEMORY BANK

THE GRAND FAMILY:

THE GRANDCHILDREN

To be lucky enough to know them…and to be a part of their lives…!
What are some of the memories that you have when your mind wanders back to holidays, vacations, times together, times apart, family rituals…

_____

_____

_____

_____

_____

_____

_____

_____

_____

_____

THE GRAND FAMILY:

THE GRANDCHILDREN

THE MEMORY BANK

MORE FAMILY:

AUNTS, UNCLES, AND COUSINS

Recall some of the times that bring a smile or a chuckle.

_____

_____

_____

_____

_____

_____

_____

_____

_____

_____

_____

_____

FAMILY:
AUNTS, UNCLES, AND COUSINS

THE MEMORY BANK

ALMOST LIKE FAMILY:

FRIENDS

They often know you...the real you. Share the good times. Remember when...?

_____

_____

_____

_____

_____

_____

_____

_____

_____

_____

_____

_____

_____

ALMOST LIKE FAMILY:
FRIENDS

IMPORTANT-TO-ME PEOPLE

When something does happen to you, it will be necessary to notify those near and far who are dear to you.

After all, you don't want your college friend in Indiana to be mad at you for not sending her a birthday card. She may have no idea that you have checked out...

Use this space to write down those names and phone numbers that are in your head.

Name	Address	Phone Number

IMPORTANT-TO-ME PEOPLE

Name	Address	Phone Number

NOT-TO-BE FORGOTTEN SPECIAL DATES:
IMPORTANT BIRTHDAYS, ANNIVERSARIES...

Name	Address/Phone Number	Special Day

MORE NOT-TO-BE FORGOTTEN SPECIAL DATES:
IMPORTANT BIRTHDAYS, ANNIVERSARIES...

Name	Address/Phone Number	Special Day

PHOTOGRAPHS —
VIDEOS —
& AUDIO TAPES

Do you have photographs?

Where are they? Is there some sort of rhyme or reason to them or are they heaped in a box?

Are the people in the photo identified? Are the photos dated?

Do you have videos that preserve your memories of the birthday parties, the vacations, the swim team championships?

I ask these very simple questions because sometimes they need to be asked.

You cannot go back in time and take that perfect picture. Things and people change so quickly, don't miss out.

Have a family photo taken yearly – include the pets.

If one person tends to be the photographer in your group, let them come out from behind the camera and be a part of the picture.

You won't be sorry.

PHOTOGRAPHS —
VIDEOS —
& AUDIO TAPES

PHOTOGRAPHS:

Can be found: _____

_____

_____

VIDEOS:

Can be found: _____

_____

_____

AUDIO TAPES:

Can be found: _____

_____

_____

THE OTHER CHILDREN – THE PETS

Pet's Name: _____

Nickname: _____

Favorite Food/Treats: _____

_____

Medication: _____

Favorite Toys: _____

_____

Sleeping Arrangements: _____

Favorite Play/Exercise: _____

_____

Vet's Name: _____

Address: _____ Phone: _____

Papers can be found: _____

Who would you like to continue the care of your baby? Name: _____

Address:_____ Phone: _____

THE OTHER CHILDREN – THE PETS

Pet's Name: _____

Nickname: _____

Favorite Food/Treats: _____

_____

Medication: _____

Favorite Toys: _____

_____

Sleeping Arrangements: _____

Favorite Play/Exercise: _____

_____

Vet's Name: _____

Address: _____ Phone: _____

Papers can be found: _____

Who would you like to continue the care of your baby? Name: _____

Address: _____ Phone: _____

JUST BETWEEN YOU AND ME...

For a man who has done his natural duty, death is as natural and welcome as sleep.

George Santayana

THE CHILDREN

It's the little things that will be most important to remember and keep up.

Child's Name: _____

Child's Nickname: _____

Birthday: _____

Special Health Concerns: _____

_____

_____

Allergies/Medications: _____

_____

_____

Doctor's Name: _____

Address:_____ Phone Number:_____

Doctor's Name: _____

Address: _____ Phone Number: _____

Dentist's Name: _____

Address: _____ Phone Number: _____

THE CHILDREN

Favorite Breakfast:

Favorite Lunch:

Favorite Supper:

Favorite Snacks:

Bedtime Rituals:

Hobbies/Interests:

Favorite Books:

Fears:

Other Little Things To Remember:

THE CHILDREN

It's the little things that will be most important to remember and keep up.

Child's Name: _____

Child's Nickname: _____

Birthday: _____

Special Health Concerns: _____

_____

_____

Allergies/Medications: _____

_____

_____

Doctor's Name: _____

Address:_____ Phone Number: _____

Doctor's Name: _____

Address: _____ Phone Number: _____

Dentist's Name: _____

Address: _____ Phone Number: _____

THE CHILDREN

Favorite Breakfast:

Favorite Lunch:

Favorite Supper:

Favorite Snacks:

Bedtime Rituals:

Hobbies/Interests:

Favorite Books:

Fears:

Other Little Things To Remember:

THE CHILDREN

It's the little things that will be most important to remember and keep up.

Child's Name: _____

Child's Nickname: _____

Birthday: _____

Special Health Concerns: _____

_____

_____

Allergies/Medications: _____

_____

_____

Doctor's Name: _____

Address: _____ Phone Number: _____

Doctor's Name: _____

Address: _____ Phone Number: _____

Dentist's Name: _____

Address: _____ Phone Number: _____

THE CHILDREN

Favorite Breakfast:

Favorite Lunch:

Favorite Supper:

Favorite Snacks:

Bedtime Rituals:

Hobbies/Interests:

Favorite Books:

Fears:

Other little things to remember:

A LETTER TO MY CHILD

- Children are always curious about the facts and feelings their parents had regarding their arrival into this world.
- Here is an opportunity to share your thoughts.

Dear _____

I remember when I found out I was going to have you in my life…

The day you were born…

The things that make me smile when I look back…

A LETTER TO MY CHILD...

What I want you to know for all time...

These are my hopes and dreams for you...

A LETTER TO MY CHILD

· Children are always curious about the facts and feelings their parents had regarding their arrival into this world.
· Here is an opportunity to share your thoughts.

Dear _____

I remember when I found out I was going to have you in my life…

The day you were born…

The things that make me smile when I look back…

A LETTER TO MY CHILD...

What I want you to know for all time...

These are my hopes and dreams for you...

A LETTER TO MY CHILD

Children are always curious about the facts and feelings their parents had regarding their arrival into this world. Here is an opportunity to share your thoughts.

Dear _____

I remember when I found out I was going to have you in my life...

The day you were born...

The things that make me smile when I look back...

A LETTER TO MY CHILD...

What I want you to know for all time...

These are my hopes and dreams for you...

HAVE I EVER TOLD YOU?

If you were suddenly told that this was to be your last 30 minutes on this planet…
Who would you call?…What would you say? Think about it for a minute, you may surprise yourself.

Perhaps it is someone who has helped you become who you are. How about saying "Thank you…"?

☏ _____

" _____

_____

_____

_____

_____

_____

_____

_____

_____ "

HAVE I EVER TOLD YOU?

If you were suddenly told that this was to be your last 30 minutes on this planet…
Who would you call?…What would you say? Think about it for a minute, you may surprise yourself.

Perhaps it is someone who has helped you become who you are. How about saying "Thank you…"?

☏ _____

" _____

_____

_____

_____

_____

_____

_____

_____

_____ "

LOOKING BACK...AND LOOKING FORWARD

We're all in this together – by ourselves.

Lily Tomlin
New York Times (September 12, 1976)

THINGS I SHOULD HAVE DONE…REGRETS AND LOST OPPORTUNITIES

"Don't waste your time chasing dust."

My Mother

Let your mind wander.
Don't think about limits – money, time, distance.
If you could have done anything, what would it have been?

Would it have been art classes, parachuting, travel, volunteering your time?

THINGS I SHOULD HAVE DONE...

THINGS I AM HOPING TO GET DONE

Do it.

Now.

Find a way!

_____

_____

_____

_____

_____

_____

_____

_____

_____

_____

THINGS I AM HOPING TO GET DONE...

PREPARATION FOR THE BIG DAY

The old neighborhood has changed.
Hurley Brothers Funeral Home is now called Death 'n' Things.

Elmore Leonard

PREPARING A LAST WILL & TESTAMENT

Death is not the end; there remains the litigation.

Ambrose Bierce (1842-1914)

Take the time to leave written instructions in official legal form. Don't leave the probate court or your family with the burden of sorting out your affairs in the absence of a Will.

Keep things easy – Keep things peaceful for those left behind.

CHOOSING AN EXECUTOR:

An executor is someone who will carry out the wishes of the Will.

The person you choose as the executor of your Will should be someone who is willing and able to devote time and diligence in following through with all of the paperwork that must be accurately completed. Often, the executor will work with a lawyer and/or an accountant. Also, it is important that your executor does not buckle under the pressure that the family may apply in dealing with any questionable issues in the Will.

The Executor of my Estate: _____

Address: _____

_____

Phone: _____

Where my Last Will and Testament is kept: _____

_____

PREPARING A WILL

Areas to cover in the will: _____

_____

_____

_____

_____

_____

Questions to ask the lawyer: _____

_____

_____

_____

_____

_____

_____

_____

PREPARING A LIVING WILL

By medicine life may be prolonged, yet death will seize the doctor too.

Shakespeare

A Living Will allows your preferences to be known regarding life-sustaining treatment to prolong your life using such equipment as a ventilator. You may not want to "be kept alive" for any additional length of time – be it an extra hour, day, week or month.

The following is an example of what a Living Will states in case you are comatose, demented or terminally ill:

> If the time comes when I am incapacitated to the point when I can no longer actively take part in decisions for my own life, and am unable to direct my physician as to my own medical care, I wish this statement to stand as a testament of my wishes. I, your name, request that I be allowed to die and not to be kept alive through life support systems if my condition is deemed terminal. I do not intend any direct taking of my life, but only that my dying not be unreasonably prolonged. This request is made, after careful reflection, while I am of sound mind.

Let your family, friends and doctor know what you want regarding the prolonging of your life. Give them guidelines and/or examples of situations that you think would be helpful in having them better understand your feelings on this topic.

I would like _____ to act on my behalf in case the occasion arises in which I am not able to express my wishes directly to medical personnel.

You should contact Choice in Dying, 200 Varick St., New York 10014, Phone: 800-989-9455, Internet: www.choices.org, to find out what your own state allows.

A LIVING WILL...

Guidelines and/or examples of situations that you think would be helpful in having your family/friends better understand your feelings on the topic of prolonging your life:

_____

_____

_____

_____

_____

_____

_____

_____

_____

_____

_____

_____

EVERYTHING YOU WANTED TO KNOW ABOUT CASKETS AND FUNERALS BUT WERE AFRAID TO ASK

Difficult and sometimes costly decisions have to made quickly, often under great emotional stress. You do not have to leave these decisions for others to make.

So here is the scoop from the Federal Trade Commission regarding caskets and burial vaults so you can make an informed decision after you know the facts:

- A casket is frequently the single most expensive funeral item if you are planning a traditional funeral.

- Manufacturers and funeral providers are prohibited from making claims that caskets or vaults will keep out water, dirt, and other gravesite substances when that is not true.

- Funeral providers are prohibited from telling you a particular funeral item or service can indefinitely preserve a body in the grave.

- The Funeral Rule requires funeral directors to itemize prices and provide consumers with price lists, and price information over the phone.

Sometimes manufacturers of caskets and burial vaults give to the funeral providers promotional materials that may appeal to the desire to protect the physical remains of the deceased. They may do this by making false or exaggerated claims about the durability of their products.

The Federal Trade Commission (FTC) has issued orders against some manufacturers, prohibiting them from making such false or deceptive durability claims.

CASKETS

A casket, also called a coffin, is very often the single most expensive funeral item you may have to buy if you are planning a traditional funeral. A casket is not required for a direct cremation or an immediate burial. With the latter, the body is generally buried without viewing or embalming (treating the body so as to protect from decay) and is generally placed in an alternative container made of unfinished wood, pressboard, cardboard, or canvas.

Caskets vary widely in style and price and are typically sold for their visual appeal. The terms "gasketed," "protective," and "sealer" are frequently used to describe a metal casket. These terms mean that the casket has a rubber gasket or other features that delay the penetration of water and prevent rust. These protective features add to their cost.

Unlike metal caskets, wooden caskets generally are not gasketed and do not carry a warranty for longevity. Usually manufacturers of both wooden and metal caskets warrant workmanship and materials.

BURIAL VAULTS OR GRAVE LINERS

Often, cemeteries require a burial vault or a grave liner to enclose the casket in a grave. The casket is placed into either a vault or a liner to prevent the ground from caving in as the casket deteriorates. A grave liner also called a "rough box" is made of reinforced concrete and lowered into the grave prior to burial. A burial vault is more substantial and expensive than a grave liner. It is typically sold for its visual appeal and is usually gasketed. The vault may be sold with a warranty of protective strength.

PRESERVATION AND PROTECTIVE CLAIMS

Under the FTC's Funeral Rule, funeral providers are prohibited from making claims that funeral goods, such as caskets or vaults, will keep out water, dirt, and other gravesite substances when that is not true, The Rule also prohibits funeral providers from telling you a particular funeral item or service can indefinitely preserve a body in the grave. Such claims are untrue.

PRE-PLANNING FUNERALS

The FTC's Funeral Rule requires funeral directors to itemize prices and provide consumers with price lists, and price information over the phone, which are essential for comparing costs. If you are considering prearranging a funeral for yourself or a loved one, ask funeral directors about the different types of dispositions and ceremonies available. At the same time, scrutinize claims made by the manufacturers of such products as caskets and burial vaults.

To get started, you can inquire in person about funeral arrangements, the funeral provider will give you a **General Price List**. This list, which you can keep, contains the cost of each individual funeral item and service offered. As with telephone inquiries, you can use this information to help select the funeral provider and funeral items you want, need, and are able to afford. The price list also discloses important legal rights and requirements regarding funeral arrangements. It must include information about embalming, caskets for cremation, and required purchases.

The Funeral Rule requires that the funeral provider gives you a **Statement of Funeral Goods and Services Selected** after you select the goods and services you would like. The statement combines in one place the prices of the individual items you are considering for purchase, as well as the total price.

Here are a number of issues to consider when thinking about prepaying for funeral goods and services:

- Be sure you know what you are paying for. Are you purchasing merchandise and/or services?
- What happens to money you have prepaid?
- What happens to the interest income on money that is prepaid and put into a trust account?
- Are you protected if the firm goes out of business?
- Can you cancel the contract and get your money back if you change your mind?
- What if you should move to a different area? Can you transfer your services?

Keep copies of any documents that you sign or that you are given when these prearrangements are made. It is important that family members or friends know of such plans.

REQUIRED PURCHASES:

You do not have to purchase unwanted goods or services or pay any fees as a condition to obtaining those products and services you do want, other than one permitted fee for services of the funeral director and staff, and fees for other goods and services selected by you or required by state law.

UNDER THE FUNERAL RULE:

- You have the right to choose only the funeral goods and services you want, with some exceptions.

- The funeral provider must disclose this right in writing on the general price list.

- The funeral provider must disclose on your itemized statement of goods and services selected the specific state law that requires you to purchase any particular item.

- The funeral provider may not refuse, or charge a fee, to handle a casket you purchased elsewhere.

The facts that were compiled here came straight from the Federal Trade Commission's brochures on the topics of funerals and caskets and burial vaults. If you want these brochures, you can contact: Public Reference, Federal Trade Commission, Washington, D.C. 20580, phone: (202) 326-2222.

There is nothing to stop you from calling various funeral homes in your area and asking for their General Price List. Your are now armed with the facts from the Big Boys – the FTC.

This way you can take a look at what is offered and what you need and want based on the budget you had in mind.

THE FINAL DRESS REHEARSAL

This is what I would like:

DISPOSITION OF MY BODY:

Cremation:

☐ Direct cremation which is cremation of the deceased without a viewing or other ceremony at which the body is present

☐ Cremation after a ceremony

Donate my organs:

☐ Organ donor card or sticker on motor vehicle license

Donate my body:

☐ To a medical or educational institution:

   ☐ Directly

   ☐ After a ceremony

Immediate Burial – no viewing/no embalming (unless required by law)

Memorial Service to be held at: _____

Street _____ City _____ State _____

Phone _____

Funeral with Viewing

Wake :   To be held at: Name _____

Street _____ City _____ State _____

Casket : ☐ Open   ☐ Closed

Flowers: _____

Musical Selections to be played while family is receiving guests:

_____

_____

_____

Pallbearers: _____

_____

Clergy of choice: _____

What Shall I Wear? _____

Person in Charge of Arrangements: Name: _____

Address: _____

City/State/Zip: _____

Phone: _____ Relationship: _____

LOCATION, LOCATION, LOCATION

Where will you finally hang your hat?

CREMATION:

In an urn of my choosing: _____

To be held in a place of honor located: _____

or Scatter my ashes – Where: _____

      By whom: _____

      Special requests: _____

      _____

      _____

OR **EARTH BURIAL:**

in a plot located in:

Cemetery Name: _____

Street: _____ Town: _____

County: _____ Country: _____

Plot Location: _____

Deed is located: _____

OR **MAUSOLEUM:**

Name: _____

Street: _____ Town: _____

County: _____ Country: _____

Contact Name: _____

MY MARKER comes in the form of:

    A Flat Marker: _____

    A Stone:

        Size: _____

        Style: _____

    If you are a veteran of the military, you are entitled to a marker which lies at the foot of the grave:

        Would you like to have this marker?   ☐ Yes   ☐ No

MY EPITAPH will read:

_____

_____

_____

YOUR FINAL PRESS RELEASE...YOUR OBITUARY

Think of your obituary as a press release of sorts...well, it is, you know.

Full Name: _____

Birthday: _____

Address: (Present/Previous): _____

_____

_____

_____

Family Relations: _____

_____

_____

_____

_____

_____

_____

_____

Employment History:

_____

_____

_____

_____

_____

Organizations/Affiliations:

_____

_____

_____

_____

_____

Charitable Donations to be made in your name:

_____

_____

_____

_____

Newspapers to be Notified: _____

THE BIG DAY ARRIVES

*No matter how rich you become, how famous or powerful,
when you die the size of your funeral will still pretty much depend on the weather.*

Michael Pritchard

THE COMMAND PERFORMANCE – THE CEREMONY

THE SERVICE:

Place: _____

Street: _____ City:_____

County:_____ State: _____ Country:_____

MUSIC:
Music is very important to set the mood and feeling. Select some songs that would reflect your essence and personality.

_____

_____

_____

_____

PRAYERS AND/OR SPECIAL REQUESTS:

_____

_____

_____

_____

THE CEREMONY

ADDITIONAL THOUGHTS (Flowers, Prayer cards, Gathering after the burial etc.)**:**

_____

_____

_____

_____

_____

_____

_____

_____

_____

_____

_____

_____

_____

_____

PARTING WORDS TO BE READ AT THE FINAL SERVICE

To send those you love off with a smile on their face, here is your chance to bring some peace and closure.

Here are four possibilities for starting this piece:

"You know I always liked to have the last word…so, here it is!…"

or

"I guess you know why we're here…"

or

"I never liked being the center of attention, but…here we are…"

or

"Don't cry for me…"

PARTING WORDS

IN CLOSING

It matters not how a man dies, but how he lives.

Samuel Johnson

BECAUSE YOU TOOK JUST A FEW MINUTES OF YOUR TIME...

Even if you just filled out one little section in this working book, you have helped someone you love at a time when they need it most. You might have helped yourself.

For someone else as well as you yourself to know what you want in life and death will bring everyone peace of mind.

I knew when all was said and done that I did all that I could have for my parents.

And I did it – their way.

Right down to my father's map to the septic tank. The yard was never dug up in search of the tank.

Use this book as your map – so your loved ones don't have to go digging.

P.S. Don't forget to let someone know that you have this workbook and where they may find it in your absence.

That someone you would like to know about this workbook is:

Name: _____

Street: _____

City: _____ State: _____ Zip: _____

County: _____ Country: _____

Phone: _____

ADDITIONAL NOTES AND UPDATES

ADDITIONAL NOTES AND UPDATES

ADDITIONAL NOTES AND UPDATES

ADDITIONAL NOTES AND UPDATES

ADDITIONAL NOTES AND UPDATES

ADDITIONAL NOTES AND UPDATES

ADDITIONAL NOTES AND UPDATES

Every family has their favorite little story…

As we travel around this country talking about "In the Checklist of Life", people share wonderful stories about favorite hiding places, family traditions, interesting services – things that make their family unique. Everyone has a story to tell.

We all learn from one another. We all learn from experience.

We would like to hear from you. As you went through the various sections of this workbook, what stories, thoughts and words of wisdom came to mind? Please share them with us.

You may mail them to us at AAIP Publishing, P.O. Box 102, Rockfall, CT 06481 or e-mail at lynn@connix.com or visit our website at http://www.checklistoflife.com. Please include your name, address and phone number and e-mail address.

We are looking forward to hearing from you!

There is a destiny that makes us brothers;

None goes his way alone –

All that we send into the lives of others

Comes back into our own.

Special Words from a Special Person

BECAUSE YOU ASKED FOR IT...
WE HAVE IT!

EXPANDABLE FILE FOLDER

IDEAL FOR KEEPING EVERYTHING IN ONE PLACE!

Store this workbook and your important papers all in one place!

This 6-pocket file folder is made of strong polypropylene
and has a front flap with button for closing.

Your documents will stay organized, clean and secure.

JUST $9.95 PLUS S/H ($4.00)

TO ORDER:

CALL

TOLL-FREE
WITH YOUR VISA OR
MASTERCARD
**7 DAYS A WEEK
24 HOURS A DAY**
1-888-800-6446